Wisdom Shots

GRISELDA PINTO

BLUEROSE PUBLISHERS
India | U.K.

Copyright © Griselda Pinto 2023

All rights reserved by author. No part of this publication may be reproduced, stored in a retrieval system or transmitted in any form or by any means, electronic, mechanical, photocopying, recording or otherwise, without the prior permission of the author. Although every precaution has been taken to verify the accuracy of the information contained herein, the publisher assumes no responsibility for any errors or omissions. No liability is assumed for damages that may result from the use of information contained within.

BlueRose Publishers takes no responsibility for any damages, losses, or liabilities that may arise from the use or misuse of the information, products, or services provided in this publication.

For permissions requests or inquiries regarding this publication, please contact:

BLUEROSE PUBLISHERS
www.BlueRoseONE.com
info@bluerosepublishers.com
+91 8882 898 898
+4407342408967

ISBN: 978-93-5819-983-3

First Edition: December 2023

*Dedicated to my beloved parents,
the late Eddie and Doreen Dias....*

Contents

Foreword viii
Acknowledgments xi
Disclaimer xiii
Introduction xv

1 Who Am I?.. 1
2 The Greatest Power is Within Me..................................... 2
3 Conquer the unconquerable... 4
4 The Present is a Gift... 5
5 Lifeline Support.. 6
6 Strength of a Woman... 7
7 It's a Beautiful World.. 8
8 Living on Hope.. 9
9 It is All in my Hands.. 10
10 An Encounter with Fear... 11
11 Reaching for the Stars... 13
12 The World in a Spot of Mud... 14
13 Together into the Sunset... 16
14 Write to Heal.. 17
15 Eyes That Don't See.. 18
16 Let Passion Power You.. 20

17	Encircled in Love	21
18	Let People Be	23
19	Oh, to sleep like a baby	24
20	Stay Childlike	25
21	Slow and Steady	27
22	Self-Respect is Paramount	28
23	Humanity's Triumph	29
24	Life is Life	31
25	Man is no Machine	32
26	Soul Over Body	34
27	Still point in a turning world	36
28	Of Deepfakes and Human Accountability	38
29	When the Soul Takes Over	40
30	Money Can't Buy Love	41
31	To Forgive is Divine	43
32	Wake up!	45
33	Tact Works!	47
34	Growing in Love	48
35	The Greatest Love of All	49
36	Kindness: The Supreme Virtue	50
37	Art Therapy	51
38	When your Heart Smiles	53
39	The Walking Dead	54
40	Chocolate Friendship	56
41	When a soul mate dies	58
42	Happy Relationships Are an Inside Job	60
43	A Make-believe World	61
44	Excuse Me, Please	62
45	Pigeons Outside My Window	64

46 Lukewarm, not OK, Please 65
47 Let it Be 67
48 Learning to Let Go 69
49 Double Standards 70
50 Who am I? 72

Reviews 74

Foreword

When I first had the privilege of meeting Griselda Pinto in the context of our professional lives, her qualities immediately left an indelible mark on me. With a pragmatic demeanor, unwavering focus, and profound humility, Griselda embodied the quintessential corporate professional, possessing an innate sense of responsibility and an unwavering work ethic.

Over the passage of years, I bore witness to the myriad chapters of her life unfolding - the sacred vows of marriage, the profound experience of falling in love, the joys of motherhood, the heartache of bidding farewell to her cherished parents, and her graceful navigation through diverse phases, at times with effortless grace and at others, with unwavering determination. It was during these transformative years that I observed Griselda evolve into a multifaceted individual, her core imbued with a deep wellspring of sensitivity and empathy.

One cannot deny that gaining a thorough understanding of another person's mind is a challenging feat without access to their innermost thoughts or deep reflections. It was only by reading her exceptional book, filled with her reflections and insights, that I was able to uncover the profound beauty of her intellectual world.

Her book serves as a metaphorical flame, dancing spiritedly in the wind, sparking contemplation about the simplicity inherent in life's ordinary moments. It beckons us to behold something distinct, something transcendent, something profoundly enriching - an experience that reshapes us at the very core of our being.

I came to understand, through Griselda's insights, the paramount significance of infusing our lives with love, positivity, and happiness through the small, often overlooked, gestures. Yet, true to her inherently pragmatic disposition, she underscores the importance of staying engaged and productive, of ardently pursuing our dreams, and of translating those aspirations into tangible reality through unyielding dedication, relentless perseverance, and unswerving hard work.

Perhaps the most compelling message that resonated with me within the pages of her book was her unwavering conviction that while our work may not singularly define our identity, our attitude toward work undeniably shapes the essence of who we are. This profound revelation acted as a catalyst, propelling me to bid adieu to procrastination and to stand resolute in the face of adversity. Far too often, I found myself on the cusp of surrendering to the formidable challenges life presented. Griselda's reflections illuminated the path of the growth mindset - the unwavering belief that nothing is beyond reach when we earnestly strive for it. Her book infused me with a renewed sense of purpose, and I am confident it will serve as a wellspring of motivation for countless others, igniting the flame of inner strength and determination when faced with daunting obstacles. Nothing is insurmountable.

When Griselda initially confided in me about her aspirations to pen this book, her apprehensions about its fate in an era dominated by instant gratification through social media were palpable. Yet, I harbored unwavering confidence in her ability to deliver excellence, grounded in her approach to both work and life. She believes that life is fleeting and we must leave a meaningful impact. She is a firm believer in the principle that if we do not positively influence and impact others, we risk living a life devoid of purpose, akin to crossing the finish line with only a physical shell, void of the soul. Fueled by such potent motivations for the greater good, I recognized that Griselda was destined for exceptional accomplishments.

My role, consequently, metamorphosed into that of an ardent supporter, tirelessly cheering her on as she diligently crafted her 50 pearls of wisdom - a seemingly modest number in comparison to her vast reservoir of insights into facets of life that often evade our conscious thought.

In this self-help book, Griselda presents her perspective on various life events and individuals in an anecdotal style. Her passion for writing, pursued as both a leisurely pursuit and a vocation, gives her words a captivating potency. Her writing is a harmonious blend of humility, ease, equilibrium, grace, empathy, and profound sensitivity.

With enviable simplicity, Griselda artfully navigates the complexities of different dimensions of life, subtly imparting invaluable lessons along the way. Her unique outlook is akin to a breath of fresh air, providing something of significance for every reader to glean from her book. It would be a formidable task not to emerge from these pages with a heightened sense of wisdom - truly a repository of precious gems.

Varsha Khanna

Ex-Journalist, Features – Business Standard. Currently Writer, Editor, Teacher, Mother

Acknowledgments

In the journey of bringing this book to life, there have been numerous individuals whose contributions and support have been invaluable. I want to express my deep gratitude and appreciation to all of them.

Varsha Khanna, thank you for writing the foreword to this book. Your kindness, unwavering confidence in my abilities, and covert mentorship have been a marvellous source of inspiration throughout the journey of this book. Our discussions on life and analysis of perspectives helped fine-tune my lens on a couple of occasions while writing the book.

I also extend my heartfelt thanks to Pranati Mehta, a dear friend of many years, who, despite her busy schedule as an art teacher at the American School of Mumbai, gave her valuable inputs to the cover design and helped in the final selection.

To my well-wishers over the years, Brenda Fernandes, Director-HR at Compunnel Inc., NY; Pratap Antony, Marketing Communications Strategy Consultant, Rio Castellino, Founder of Teams R US, and all my silent supporters. Your support, in various ways, has played a significant role in my journey of words. Your belief in my work has been a constant source of motivation.

I want to express my sincere gratitude to Mario Poppen whose generosity of spirit is a rare gem in today's world. I deeply appreciate your willingness to contribute a few words to this book dedicated to my loving parents, who were friends of yours.

A special thanks to Parneet Kaur, Associate Vice President, Marketing, Sony Pictures Network India and recent *BW Marketing World's 'Marketers 40 under 40'* awardee for providing me with a glowing comment for the book. Parneet, you have consistently had my best interests at heart and have been a staunch supporter of the "Can do" winning spirit over the years. Much gratitude.

Special acknowledgment to Fr. Antony Charangat for taking time out of his busy schedule to share his thoughts. Your insights are invaluable, and I am honoured by your involvement in this project.

Last but certainly not least, I want to convey my deep and heartfelt gratitude to Suma Varughese, the ex-editor of *Life Positive and Society* magazines and author of *50 Life Lessons and Travelling Light and Travelling Lighter*. Despite your hectic schedule, your willingness to edit this book has been a true blessing.

To all those mentioned here and to the countless others who have supported me on this literary journey, thank you for being a part of this endeavor. Your contributions have made this book a reality.

With gratitude,
Griselda

Disclaimer

This book is intended to provide anecdotal insights, experiences, and personal observations related to self-help and personal growth. The content contained within this book is presented for informational and entertainment purposes only. The author is not a licenced therapist, counsellor, or professional in the field of psychology or personal development.

Some of the experiences shared in this book may be based on real-life events, while others are fictional or altered for illustrative purposes.

The characters, scenarios, and situations depicted are created for the purpose of illustrating personal growth and self-improvement concepts, and any resemblance of these to real individuals, living or deceased, or specific events is purely coincidental.

The information and advice presented in this book should not be considered a substitute for professional guidance, therapy, or medical advice. It is essential to consult with qualified experts, such as mental health professionals or medical practitioners, when dealing with personal or mental health issues.

Readers are encouraged to exercise critical judgement and discretion when applying any of the content from this book to their own lives. The author and publisher are not responsible for any consequences or outcomes resulting from the implementation of the concepts, ideas, or suggestions presented herein.

The reader assumes full responsibility for their actions and decisions, and any reliance on the information within this book is done at their own risk. The author and publisher do not guarantee the accuracy or effectiveness of any strategies or techniques described in this book. Individual results may vary, and there are no explicit or implied promises of specific outcomes or achievements.

This book is not intended as a comprehensive guide to self-help and personal growth, and it may not address every individual's unique circumstances or needs. The content is reflective of the author's personal opinions and should be interpreted as such.

By reading this book, the reader acknowledges and accepts the terms of this disclaimer and agrees to use the information provided here responsibly and at their own discretion.

Introduction

I hope my diary will help anyone who stumbles upon it or has been gifted a copy. For in its pages are life truths that have arisen through reflection, and these may nudge you to look at life through a deeper perspective than is visible at face value.

They began as intimate, personal experiences, but in retrospect, they converged into a cohesive worldview that has made my life's journey more significant.

The common thread that holds this collection together is its plea to lead a kinder, simpler, and more conscious life. To rise above the material plane, to care for one another, to cherish relationships, to celebrate life, and to periodically introspect on where we are going and why. I may be one among many voices to advocate a more conscious life, but in a world that seems hurtling towards doom and destruction, every word of wisdom helps.

I was born into a middle-class family with parents who showered me with love and affection, so much so that I can confidently say that if there is any good in me, it is attributable to the wonderful nurturing they gave me as long as they were alive. This has given me moorings, and a capacity to write from the heart, and to search for the truth in the ordinary happenings of life.

I make no claims to be a sage or a savant, yet I hope this diary is not entirely devoid of merit. The book would have accomplished its purpose if it has helped spark your imagination, and ignite a deeper evolution within you.

Writing each of them was like getting a sensory massage. My eyes, ears and heart feel awakened, put to better use and in the process, I have acquired a more balanced mind. This has helped me tremendously in every interaction, whether at home, at work, or in the company of family and friends.

I am leaving some blank pages in this book for you to write down your own observations of life, with the hope it will inspire you to live life more deeply and meaningfully.

Happy reading!
Griselda Pinto

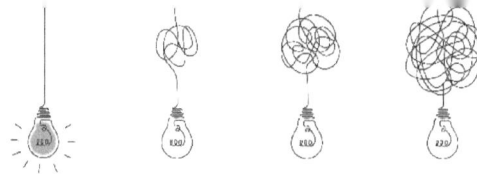

#1
Who Am I?

I feel like a two-faced Janus.

Cosmetics and technology are surreptitiously transforming me into somebody else, coating me with a fake identity. This dawned on me when my daughter pointed out that I looked beautiful even without makeup. It made me realise the needless time and energy I had devoted to creating an alter image when I was already good enough. So desperate was I to fit into world standards that I was even using technology liberally and unfailingly to add pizzazz to my photos before sharing them with the world on social media. I was indefatigable in my attempt to make myself several shades more attractive than my natural self, which I thought of as plain and not good enough.

As a result, two versions of myself were coexisting in disharmony. One was a digitally transformed me to dazzle the world, and the other was the real me, warts and all.

But isn't the real me enough for this fleeting world?

#2
The Greatest Power is Within Me

If life throws me a challenge, getting beaten down is not an option.

Years ago, when I had little option but to quit my full-time, lucrative career to tend to my school-going children, it was a tough decision to make. I had felt trapped in a dreadful quandary.

If I stayed on at work, I knew my children wouldn't get the nurturing they so rightly deserved, and if I quit, I would be throwing up a profitable career and missing out on the best years of going up the career ladder.

On the day I eventually turned in my papers, I remember feeling desolate and uncertain. I closed my eyes, wondering if I had made the right choice. And then I heard a soft, gentle voice egging me on. It urged me to believe in myself, tap into the immense power of the mind, and look for a middle path. To doggedly confront the crippling fear of change and vanquish the adversary of negativity.

Feeling refreshed and renewed, I opened my eyes slowly and experienced a breathtaking rejuvenation, as one does after frolicking beneath a cascading waterfall.

Ever since this episode, I have begun to see obstructions as possible windows of opportunity with a mature awareness that changes are an inevitable part of life, and breaking out of our comfort zone is part and parcel of it. Instead of allowing changes to cripple us, let us strive to shoulder them squarely, and rise above ourselves to climb higher and higher on the ladder of life.

#3
Conquer the unconquerable

Summer can be brutal on animals. They have to brave the scorching sun, scarce water and soaring temperatures of 45 degrees.

Birds, their wings battered down by the summer heat, search desperately for water to quench their thirst. Dogs pant, and seek shade as their tongues hang out.

Survival is the name of the game; and these animals show an unflinching resolve, resilience and perseverance while searching for their sustenance.

Humans can take a cue or two from such animal behaviour when faced with situations where survival is a matter of keeping your head above water by hook or by crook. It could be a business, relationship, or a health-related crisis that may be deteriorating or breaking up to the point of no return, or it may even be a natural calamity that takes away your all. Whatever the challenge, we need to learn from our animal brethren.

Despite the temptation to give up and accept our fate, we should fight to beat the odds, even when there appears to be no visible lifeline. Nature loves courage, and it may just surprise you when you make the commitment to remove insurmountable obstacles.

Fight the "unbeatable" foe, and the Universe will pull you up rather than grind you down.

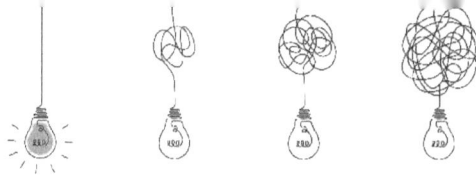

#4
The Present is a Gift

Tanya, my friend, discovered a little lump on her neck many years ago. Though she had been continually aware of it, she chose not to reveal it to a doctor for fear of it turning out to be cancerous, while hoping it would simply fly away. In December 2022, she began coughing excessively for a few weeks and was diagnosed with bronchitis. However, her cough intensified, and it was then that she showed the doctor the lump in her throat. After a series of tests, she was diagnosed with tuberculosis and was forced to undergo surgery for the removal of the lump.

If only she had taken the bull by the horns right at the onset, surgery could have been avoided.

Sadly, like her, I know many, including me, who tend to procrastinate when it comes to health problems, relationship issues or office dilemmas because doing so offers us temporary peace. But when we do this, does the problem magically disappear? Or does it grow into gigantic proportions and smack us in the face?

I now believe the more we avoid confronting a problem, the worse it will become; the more we run away from facing the situation, the more we magnify it.

Procrastination may not only be the thief of time. It could well end up stealing your life.

#5
Lifeline Support

Do what you love, dismissing what the rest of the world has to say about it.

My daughter's friend, who just turned 15, practises ballet for four hours a day without any coercion from her parents. She does so because she loves the dance. Conversations with her playmates almost always include a rhapsody on her beautiful experiences at the ballet classes. When I meet her, I am awestruck by the radiant vibe she always seems to exude.

However, she doesn't exhibit the same passion for her studies and has a tendency to feel stressed out before any school assessment. To help her cope with her anxieties during these crucial times, she makes sure she slots in some time for ballet "When I am stressed out, ballet is my life support. Even when assessments are looming over my head, I spend some time dancing to relieve my anxiety," she confides.

When we are engaged in what we are passionate about, life becomes a bed of roses, and we experience a bouquet of happiness. This passion can also help us tide over difficult times and forget worries that would normally consume us.

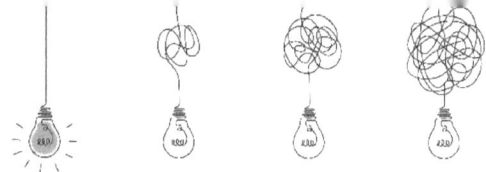

#6
Strength of a Woman

She was the picture of calm after the storm.

The other day, while commuting by train, I found myself seated across a pretty, young, slim girl in her 20s. She seemed like any girl of her age, sitting cross-legged, handbag on lap, dressed neatly, and wearing a casual, pretty, and happy demeanour. Except that the rim of her upper eyelid drooped so much that it nearly obscured her pupil and impaired her vision. The eyelid was also brutally disfigured by a deep scar. And yet, despite this distortion she was a vision of calm composure. I was struck by her resilience and Zen attitude for it was obvious she was hiding a tragic narrative of perhaps retribution, physical abuse, or an accident.

I groaned internally at life's unfairness and wondered, "What if she had chosen to be miserable and look miserable?" Instead, she exuded strength and competence as she calmly looked past the run-down settlements that lined the railways tracks and focused on the spacious sky.

I admired her queen-like composure. And how she seemed to have turned her back on sorrow. She had found a way to compress her pain until it transformed into power.

Having a positive attitude is inspirational and encouraging for others, more so when you are a victim of trials and tribulations.

#7
It's a Beautiful World

Her truth was my falsehood. I stand beautifully corrected.

I have a beautiful-looking aunt who uses the word "beautiful" very liberally and sincerely. To compliment me on my cooking, she would gush, "Oh, it was so beautiful!" She would rave about her friend's grandchildren with, "Oh! They were so beautiful!" Initially, I found this repetitive use of the word to be meaningless and fake. But one day, when I was in one of my rare contemplative moods, it occurred to me that perhaps she was viewing life through a different lens.

Perhaps I was too bogged down with worldly cares to notice the beauty of the world. Maybe she, on the other hand, was living a beautiful life. Maybe she was actively discovering true beauty in the sight, sound, smell, and taste of things.

And, really, isn't this the point of living when we have been divinely gifted a beautiful world?

Life is beautiful. We should live every moment and be happy.

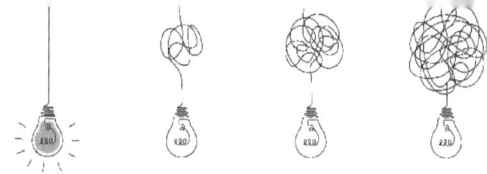

#8
Living on Hope

Even when all hope is lost, you still wait for the wordless tune of the white dove.

Turkey earthquake 2023: Of the 28,000 people killed in the deadly earthquake, the single miraculous rescue of a two-month-old baby alive in the rubble after 120 hours instilled hope in the shattered hearts of men.

Hope is a good thing for a man begins to die when he ceases to expect anything from tomorrow.

#9
It is All in my Hands

I was passing by a construction site. Women were carrying stones on their heads. An infant lying in a cloth cradle under the hot sun woke up and started crying. The young mother ran to her son's side. Watching the ordinary sight of her work-worn hands rocking her infant to sleep was an inspiration.

Any work, whether blue collar or white collar, whether housework or office work, when done sincerely, is sacred and uplifting. Yet sometimes people choose not to work, happy with handouts of ancestral wealth, failing to realise their potential, to contribute to the world, or develop their self-worth.

In a real sense, are they not truly poor?

Being rich isn't only about money. True wealth is measured not by what you have, but by who you are.

#10
An Encounter with Fear

I was a nervous wreck, almost collapsing on the Seven Islands tour in Phuket, thanks to the maniacal boat driver at the steering wheel who drove us across the seven islands with astronomical speed.

It seemed in those excruciating moments that my precious life was hanging feebly in his hands as he set out on what seemed a solo mission to destroy me and the others on the boat.

There was a daredevil look in his eyes, as he stared straight ahead, not turning his head to the left or right while he wilfully manoeuvred the boat at great speed. Old and young passengers had to clutch on to their seats to prevent toppling over one another. The twists and turns at the wheel were so rough that we literally felt the sea splashing fountains of water on our faces from both sides of the boat.

My 12-year-old daughter, seated to my right, winced as I gripped her hand as tightly as I could, and chided me for my skittishness. Neither the calm smiles of the more seasoned passengers, nor the charming banter of the skipper who seemed unaffected by the rocking, could soothe my nerves.

Yet, strangely, as we eventually approached one of the islands, I slowly began to unwind and enjoy the experience.

When I look back at this incident I believe my ordeal was made memorable and adventurous by the driver's defiance and my ability to confront my anxieties. Looking back, I wouldn't have wanted it any other way.

I felt empowered to have been there and done it.

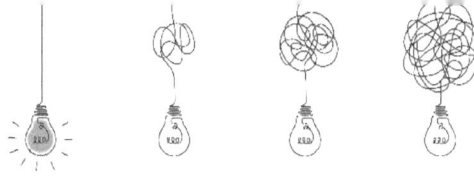

#11
Reaching for the Stars

The glitter of the stars can be more than just eye-catching.

We know the story of wrestler Geeta Phogat, who used to get up early in the brittle cold of the morning, have a cold bath, and practise wrestling under the supervision of her father, who was determined that she storm into the male bastion of wrestling. She ultimately won medal after medal, overcoming all the hurdles that came her way. What do these super achievers have in common? How is it that they can strive day in and day out for their goals?

I wonder if their secret to success lies in watching the stars and seeing themselves running away with them.

#12
The World in a Spot of Mud

I was on my way from the airport to my home in South Bombay after returning from Paris, which had captivated me with its splendour and intriguing culture.

Paris was a sight to behold. Those beautiful and fashionable French women dressed immaculately in smart black suits, puffing on cigarettes as they strode to their offices or some other place at a confident and rapid pace.

The magnificent Eiffel Tower, the enormous Disney World, the open excursion boat trip along the River Seine where I watched couples kiss and break out into romantic carefree dances, the wide roadways that hosted high couture fashion boutiques – all of this and more is eternally etched in my memory.

Paris reeked of sophistication and artistic beauty.

And now here I was, back in Mumbai. On my ride home, I made mental notes on the contrast between the two cities. How different they were in terms of infrastructure, dress, vibe, and language.

As I looked out of my taxi window, I happened to see a group of street children, jumping excitedly as they played marbles in a patch of mud outside their rundown shanties.

Their faces wore the glow of a good night's sleep and their bare feet seemed to dance in the shadow of the early morning sun. Despite their unwashed faces and tangled hair, their faces seemed to be lit magnificently with an inexplicable energy emanating from deep within their souls.

They looked so free and happy and gorgeously raw, as if all that they wanted out of life was theirs for the picking.

I wanted to laugh and cry at the same time. Isn't life astonishing?

While some people choose to travel thousands of miles to see the world, others remain in their own patch, and see the world in a spot of mud.

Happiness is a state of mind. And it follows the heart. Money does not enter the equation.

#13
Together into the Sunset

The other day when I was purchasing my weekly meats from Joseph's in Bandra, my eyes fell on an elderly couple, probably in their late 70s or early 80s. Unsteady on their feet, the man and his wife were holding hands as they gingerly walked down the shop's steps like two young lovers, having finished what they came to do.

Their frail bodies and grey hair gave them an air of dignity, and it all seemed to be like a scene from an enchanting, slow-motion film about love, companionship, and caring.

They did not seem to want any help – comfortable in the knowledge that they had each other, and would take things one day at a time.

The beauty of a quiet enduring relationship is magnificent. It is proof that life does not grow dimmer in the evening of our lives, and that the best years are still ahead of us.

#14
Write to Heal

When I found myself wrapped up in knots that seemed to throttle me, chaos in my head, turbulence in my heart, and a bleak future ahead, the feel of pen to paper was releasing and empowering all at once.

I took to therapeutic writing after I experienced injustice at the workplace meted out by a woman supervisor. I felt cheated because although I was giving my 100 per cent at work which I loved, it wasn't being appreciated by her. She wanted me to acquiesce to her unreasonable demands, eventually making the environment too unhealthy to deliver productive work. One day, I just threw in my papers and decided to move on.

As I poured out my frustration on paper, the pain, the sorrow, and the suffering I was experiencing flowed out unrelentingly like a running tap.

The fact that I could chuck paper into a trash bin without even reading it again, was as liberating to me as a prisoner being released from jail after serving his term.

In my opinion, when we feel we are at the bottom of the barrel, we should get right down to writing. Writing can have a therapeutic effect. Through writing, we can release our emotions and uplift our spirits. The flower in us, which we thought dead, can bloom again.

#15
Eyes That Don't See

My cousin was driving from Crawford Market towards Dadar while I was seated right next to her. The maddening Mumbai traffic was getting the better of her temper and to add to her frustration the elderly taxi driver ahead of her was driving cautiously, slowing us down. Finally, she exploded, "He is so old, he should be staying at home watching TV or doing anything else instead of annoying others with his bad driving. Why is his family sending him to work?"

It was a thoughtless remark made in the heat of the moment. But it made me reflect. How easy it is for us to imagine that the world is made expressly for our benefit and that everyone should accommodate us. What about others and their needs? Take the case of our elderly taxi driver. He was surely not driving for pleasure. It was necessary for his survival. Like it or not, he had to slog from morning to evening on Mumbai's congested streets, breathing in the heavy petrol fumes. In all probability he may have had health issues that he had ignored. And if it were a serious ailment, he would not be able to pay his hospital bills but would have to say a silent goodbye to his earthly journey due to a lack of funds.

Old age isn't easy, and the hard years would have sapped the joy from his days. My cousin was relatively young and healthy, and had never known the rigours of survival. What to her was an impediment in getting where she wanted to go, was in actuality a man dedicated to looking after his family, striving to put food on the table, clothes on his family's backs and perhaps paying for his own medicines. In his small way, a hero's life.

Looking within, I realised how often I had done the same thing myself. Losing my temper, judging people, writing them off simply because what they said or did was inconvenient to me. Could I, instead, see things from their point of view ?How much more peaceful my life would be, and how much more harmonious my relationships.

#16
Let Passion Power You

My ex-maid texted me a video on WhatsApp. Her 15-year-old school-going daughter was dancing with a group of girls and boys to a Bollywood number in a training hall under the guidance of a professionally-trained dancer.

The oomph, confidence, and ability with which she was grooving to a Bollywood number would have been generally associated with privileged youngsters. She was dressed in a crop top and slim-fitting jeans and danced with a rebellious spirit, holding nothing back, simply displaying an innate skill. I found it hard to believe this was the same child who used to accompany her mother to my house and sometimes help her with utensil washing, avoiding looking at me or even uttering a single word. Her mother used to complain about how difficult it was for her girl to cope with her studies, and here she was showing excellence in an extracurricular activity.

The male teacher was outstanding. One could feel his energy as he taught the moves to these youngsters, who did their best to mirror him.

It struck me anew that every human being regardless of their socioeconomic class – rich, middle class, or poor – can possess the sun if they simply look for it.

Have you found your sun? Are you dancing in the light?

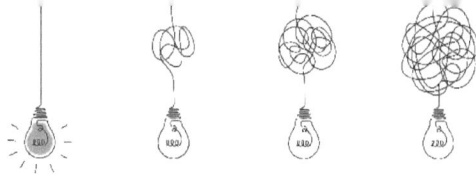

#17
Encircled in Love

I doted on my parents when they were alive. I strove hard to fulfil all their needs. It was difficult and painful to witness them in their sunset years performing ordinary tasks with extraordinary slowness. What moved me immensely, though, was how they loved each other. While my dad watched the news, my mom would be by his side, clipping out noteworthy quotes from magazines and pasting them into a scrapbook. She would enliven the atmosphere by reading him jokes she had received on her WhatsApp that she knew he would find amusing.

They would have every meal together, even if it meant that occasionally my dad had to wait until my mom returned home after a church meeting.

Their Sunday outing to my home held the same excitement for them as a trip to a foreign land would have held for us youngsters. They came to visit me dressed to the nines with a zest for life that would put many of us to shame.

They died within a month of each other – my mother first, and then my dad, -which caused me much grief.

My dad found it very difficult to believe she had truly gone. A few days after her passing, he gently told me that he believed she had gone to Australia to visit her sister and would return soon.

I recognised that I was lucky to have had a wonderful relationship with both of them and served them joyfully till the end. I now understand what it means to be blessed.

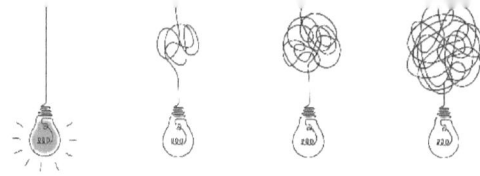

#18
Let People Be

It is difficult to remember that all five fingers are not the same size. That what makes you happy may not make another person happy. And this does not make them any less valuable than you. For example, you may have non-negotiable standards for your appearance, schooling for the children, or sticking to schedules and timelines. Someone else, on the other hand, would prefer to live life spontaneously, sleeping when they wish to, eating when they wish to, and waking up when they wish to. You may love the cappuccino at Starbucks while the other prefers drinking cutting chai from a street stall. You may love travelling but someone else is happiest at home. Nature enthrals you, for someone else, nature means nothing. While you may love to go out and have a good time, another may enjoy sitting at home with a good book.

There is no right or wrong in this. It is simply a fact to be accepted.

The more we embrace this truth, and stop fighting and trying to change the world to our liking, the more at peace we will be.

#19
Oh, to sleep like a baby

Sleep is a priceless gift to humanity. Yet many of us do not place a high value on sleep. We give it step-motherly treatment – indulging in reckless behaviour that would rupture our sleeping pattern like drinking alcohol or working late into the night, or fretting excessively.

Ask someone who is grieving the loss of a loved one, or a killer on the run, and they will tell you that they crave a tranquil slumber like a camel thirsting in the desert.

Appreciate this gift of sleep, which is as free and as valuable as the air we breathe.

#20
Stay Childlike

A nephew was down in Mumbai from Goa for selection into the All India football squad for under-17. He was a tall and athletic boy who besides being an ace at football, had a marvellous sense of humour. He could add such twists and drama to the mundane events of the day that you would be rolling on the ground with laughter.

On the weekend, we took him for a drive during which he told us about the rivalry between his team and those who were from North India. Despite their youth, he was confident of their 'power' to beat the other team. In his Konkani dialect, he mimicked his team members, the shortest and the roundest of them all. He puffed out his chest and said in Konkani: "Tim mhunntat...hanv tancho churo kortolo! (loosely translating to: "Oh, they are saying this! I will beat them to a pulp!:")

I laughed heartily at his impersonation. I had laughed this hard after a long time. It was a child's laughter, something that came from deep within me. I felt released; I was so happy, so free after a long time. I realised at that moment that responsibility had hardened me so much that I had forgotten how to laugh. I recalled my childhood days when laughing came easy.

Children make you want to start life over. They don't have a file in their minds, "All the things that could go wrong".

One must always have a childlike wonder in one's heart, even as one's worldview keeps changing. To quench the thirst for deeper love and stronger bonds, one must remember to laugh and love like a child. It is a blessing to be childlike.

Don't stop playing because you have grown old. You will grow old when you stop playing.

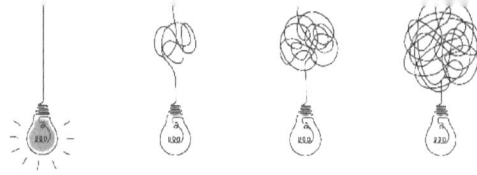

#21
Slow and Steady

Of all the self-motivational techniques I use, the one that works best for me is when I am patient with myself and keep a check on my speedometer. Like many others, I love to overpack my day with a list of things to do. But halfway to achieving my goals for the day, I give up. I realise that there isn't sufficient time in the day to finish all the tasks. So, I end up cutting them out completely.

Writing for pleasure and reading is something I want to do so much, but housework and project work get in the way, and I often end up doing neither of the two. I justify it by telling myself that in order to get value out of it, I need to invest a substantial amount of time. One day, it dawned on me that progress doesn't need me to dedicate hours to a task. Progress means consistency, so even if I were to allocate a small amount of time to the task at hand consistently, I would progress from point zero, and the results would compound over time.

After embracing this technique, I have managed to make great headway in my reading and writing habits.

The tortoise did win the race, after all.

Consistency is the moniker for success.

#22
Self-Respect is Paramount

The couple had been living separately for six years; she was working in Hong Kong and he was managing their five children back home in the Philippines. Despite being treated badly by his wife, and not receiving an ounce of money for the children's welfare, he believed she would come back to him. This hope kept him hanging on to his marriage even as he struggled to keep a happy home with his limited earnings and a 'cool' dad attitude.

He realised he needed to make a hard decision. But each time he had made up his mind to end their relationship, he was filled with a longing to plead with her to come back – which he repeatedly did, even though she adamantly refused each time. It was apparent that he was gradually losing his self-respect in the way she took his acquiescence for granted on any decision she made, and how he jumped at the opportunity to "please" her once again. To love and live on hope is one thing, and losing self-respect another.

Self-respect is everything, especially when you have lost it to someone who no longer cares about your feelings and emotions.

As Mahatma Gandhi said, "I cannot conceive of a greater loss than the loss of one's self-respect."

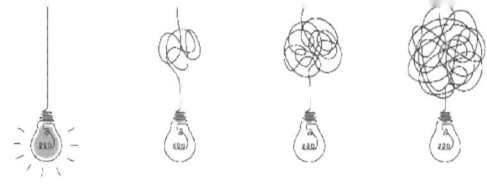

#23
Humanity's Triumph

The essence of law is justice. And in most cases, it accomplishes this. There are some circumstances, however, where the spirit of justice and truth must be followed, rather than the letter of the law.

My friend's father was facing loss in his garment business. He was deeply in debt and was not able to meet with the rising expenses. The times were so bad that he contemplated selling his house in Mumbai and moving to Ahmedabad where the cost of living would be cheaper. Each of his four sons in their late 20s, tried to help him improve the bottom line. After a few half-hearted attempts, three of them quit.

Only the youngest one continued to straddle his education and the business over the next couple of years. Whatever profits he earned, he would plough back into the business, the treatment of his father's expensive neurological condition and in the upkeep of the family home. With a single-minded focus, dedication, and extreme hard work, he was finally able to resuscitate the crashing business and make it a success. Naturally, he was the apple of his father's eye.

One day, the ailing father died; unfortunately, without leaving a will.

The family continued living together for the next few years. As they started getting married, the three elder brothers moved out.

Once they left, they started staking a claim on an equal distribution of the property. They were even willing to evict their younger brother and his family if need be, to get their portion of the wealth. They forgot the time when had it not been for the younger son's brilliance, hard work and a heartfelt desire to keep his father's house standing tall and the family name intact, they would have sunk.

Laws are normally framed to protect the rights of people. Ideally, the law should not give a right to those who haven't earned the right. And we should not be able to claim that right if we haven't worked for it, simply because the law says so.

Those that dare not grasp the thorns should never crave the rose. The spirit of the law should take precedence over the letter of the law – allowing humanity to triumph.

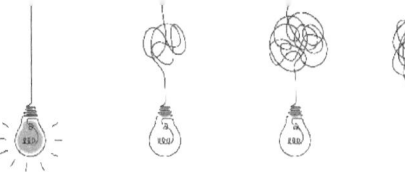

#24
Life is Life

It is when the unexpected happens, that life becomes worth living

When the job offer you thought had been withdrawn arrives knocking at your door, or when your dating partner pulls down the calendar to select a wedding date without formally proposing first. When these things happen, you realise you have been living under a cloud; the taste of sunshine feels so delicious.

You feel rejuvenated and free; life takes on a new significance. You look forward excitedly to a promising future.

These exceptional moments when life takes a turn for the better, may be few and far between but when they arrive, you want to look toward heaven, extend your arms wide, and cry out – "This is Life!".

Catch all these blessings, store them safely in the sanctuary of your heart, and never let them fade away.

The best things in life come by chance. Savour them.

#25
Man is no Machine

While lying on the operating table in a semi-anaesthetic state, a woman overheard the doctors conspiring to appropriate one of her kidneys. She tried to protest, but the words died in her mouth. Darkness enveloped her. When she woke up, she learned to her complete horror that one of her kidneys had indeed been secretly removed and the medical records altered.

These stories are unfortunately not unusual in India. We have all read stories about the nexus between unscrupulous doctors and black marketers for organ transplants. However, the atrocity exposes the bitter truth that many people fail to perceive that others are living, breathing humans with souls. They too, like us, are on a journey through life, encountering experiences that can range from the sublime to the tragic. They too, like us, have families to feed, people who love them, goals to accomplish, and dreams to fulfil. Human beings are neither statistics of the country's population, nor Covid-riddled dead bodies tightly packed in blue plastic sheets dumped into an anonymous burial ground. Most importantly, we are not bodies for doctors to cut into and rob.

We must see people as individuals with history, character, and emotions. Only that will give us the empathy that will prevent us from exploiting or abusing others. That alone will put an end to the horrific destruction caused by man's inhumanity to man. It is then that we are connected with the other's soul and therefore incapable of perceiving them as machines with number tags.

Aren't humans the crown of creation? Despite all the fatal mistakes we have committed, do we not have the potential to redeem ourselves and the planet too? Despite the fear that advances in AI will make humans redundant, the truth is that unlike us, AI is a machine.

Humans matter. Be human. And humane.

#26
Soul Over Body

The body will perish, but not the soul.

My 27-year-old gym trainer earned his six-pack body through the self-imposed army-like discipline of maintaining a strict diet, a no-excuses exercise regimen, and minimal meal cheating.

This stringent routine has helped him thrive in his physical training job and has landed him many lucrative modelling contracts. He has even got free branded gym wear and social media visibility.

One day, while our session was on, he shared about his 90-year-old grandfather.

"You know, madam, one day, I was dropping off my grandfather at a relative's place. It took him 10 minutes just to get on my motorbike! When he was younger, he was always in good shape. In fact, he was my inspiration to take up fitness as my lifestyle and my career. But that day I realised age catches up with everyone. Our bodies are machines; and the wear and tear of the machine is inevitable."

"I realised that I, too, will grow old someday, and require assistance, despite all the care I give my body. I was humbled. All the narcissistic joy I got from being ripped and toned, got tempered. I was always caring and loving with him but from that day onwards, I am patient.

He won't be with us much longer; I want to make the most of the time he has left. His body may have faded but he is still so mentally fit and emotionally beautiful. I have much to learn from him."

After all, he is a soul; who has a body.

#27
Still point in a turning world

I watched a movie recently called *Still Time*. The story revolves around a workaholic protagonist who wakes up every day to find that a year has elapsed, or a milestone has been achieved, or a life-changing event has taken place since the last time he was awake and conscious.

I think we all are guilty of leading such lives. This conundrum is especially common in working parents who are oblivious of the changes in their children. They know that their child has gone to the next grade, become taller, speaks a different vocabulary now, but suddenly one day, they see that the child has grown into an adult already.

Often, we do not see what is in sight. We do not experience even what we are currently undergoing. We do not register what is staring in our face. Much like the pictures we click, the immediate and urgent is in focus, the rest of our life is just background with bokeh. Our life is nothing more than surreal even when it seems to be the only reality we know and breathe.

What if the potter had not noticed the bumps and edges of the wet clay as he moulded it and let his pot take shape irrespective of his skill?

I can be the potter of my life. Or that of my children.

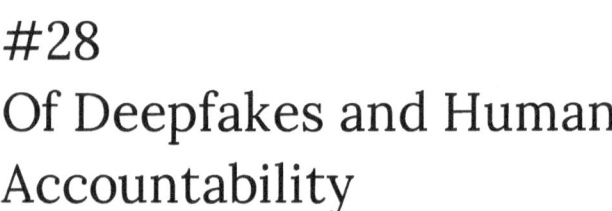

#28
Of Deepfakes and Human Accountability

As with any disruptive technology, AI too is prone to abuse as in the case of deep faking. Deep faking refers to the creation of a video or recording that has been conveniently altered to misrepresent someone as doing or saying something they have not actually done. And regulating AI to scuttle deep faking is turning into an impossible undertaking. In fact, presently AI is growing exponentially, rendering it even more simple to make convincing deep fakes.

The deep penetration of deep fakes into the real world was quite evident in the Clinton and Biden deep fake in the run-up to America's 2024 election. Their deep fake is one of thousands of movies that surfaced on social media, blending fact and fiction in the divisive realm of U.S. politics.

"I actually like Ron DeSantis a lot," Hillary Clinton reveals in a surprise online endorsement video. "He's just the kind of guy this country needs, and I really mean that."

And in another video: "Joe Biden finally lets the mask slip, unleashing a cruel rant at a transgender person." "You will never be a real woman," the president snarls.

Of course, technology is not to blame. Until human consciousness rises, there will always be humans who will exploit any new advance for their evil gains. It is analogous to the tongue which wags easily. When we use it to speak good words, it can heal relationships; when we use it to spread evil and lies, it can break them.

If we want technology to support and not hinder human progress, mankind needs to change!

#29
When the Soul Takes Over

Dance me to your beauty with a burning violin,

Dance me through the panic till I'm gathered safely in,

Lift me like an olive branch and be my homeward dove,

Dance me to the end of love

Leonard Cohen.

Sometimes when we listen to a song or read poetry, we are struck by the artist's capability to convey ordinary thoughts in an extraordinarily beautiful manner. We are quick to pin it down to his great intellect. While it is true that he may be bestowed with dollops of intelligence it is more the churning of his soul that has released such amazing work.

Quiten the intellect, and the soul will speak.

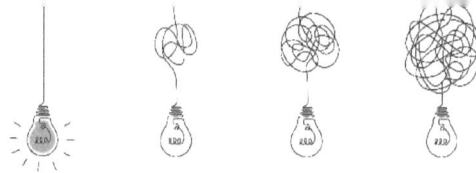

#30
Money Can't Buy Love

As working parents we might try to compensate for lost time with our children by splurging on the best car or bike we can afford for them, believing we are demonstrating our love while squelching that nagging feeling of guilt for not being available to them.

I too believed that this was adequate, until a friend related this story to me, which opened my eyes.

A wealthy father had become so preoccupied with his work that although he loved his children, he did not spend any time with them, despite the fact that he could tell they longed for him to talk to them, play cricket with them, and question them about their preparation for their exams.

In an attempt to redeem himself, on his son's 18th birthday, he gifted his son a fat cheque to buy the best car he desired. Thinking of it as proof of his love, he thought his child would be ecstatic. Besides, which 18-year-old wouldn't dream of owning a swanky car and showing it off to his friends?

But instead, brimming with anger, the boy handed him the cheque back.

"Why?" his anxious father asked.

The boy retorted furiously, "Dad, how would you feel if I gave you money for your 80th birthday but didn't make time to be there for you? You've never really been there for me, and no material gift from you, however expensive and good looking, will capture the vacant place in my heart."

Though the father was shocked at this unexpected reaction, it was a wake-up call for him. He realised that no amount of money could ever replace a father's warm love and that the priceless years lost in developing a dynamic son-father bond could only be compensated by taking corrective action.

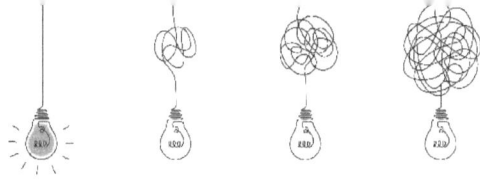

#31
To Forgive is Divine

Forgiveness is one of the hardest things to achieve, especially if you know the perpetrator won't acknowledge or accept his fault. So, we are left with two choices: either to forgive and let go, or to hold on to those difficult emotions for all time. If we decide to choose the latter, we will end up hurting ourselves needlessly. Holding on to our grudges is allowing bitterness and wrath to destroy our spirits. If it is peace and harmony we are seeking, we must make sure our souls are at peace and are pure.

Although it is difficult, forgiving someone else can be immensely liberating. I recalled being called out for "chatting" at a religious ritual, by my neighbour, a young woman in her late 30s when I was a teenager. She reprimanded me with needless hostility, even calling my parents names. This put my back up because I adored my parents. From that moment on I refused to talk to her. Over time, the hatred grew and solidified into a deep wound in my heart.

It was only after my parents died that I decided to let go of my resentment and talk to her as if the past was history.

I wasn't looking for an apology because I didn't expect to receive one. Yet, I chose to be the bigger person.

As we exchanged WhatsApp messages over some help that I needed, which she readily provided me, I felt free from the burden of harbouring all those terrible feelings I had been carrying all through these years.

I realised when you forgive, you heal, and when you let go, you grow into a better person.

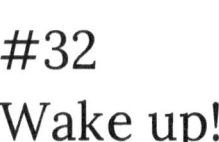

#32
Wake up!

Doctors have a dress circle view of the theatre of life and death, and it often shocks them into awakening.

A seasoned trauma surgeon with a notable reputation for successfully operating on severe cases, had an astonishing personal experience while caring for Ukrainian war victims.

While reconstructing the limbs and hands of landmine victims in Ukraine and watching people die, he realised the truth of life: Life is fleeting, wealth is pointless, and what matters most is health and peace.

"Before the war, just like everyone else, I cared much about material things in life," the surgeon admitted. "Now I understand how transient it all is. Peace and health are what matter."

Like the surgeon, for most of us, life is like a bullet-speed train, racing at breathtaking speed to an unknown destination. The momentum prevents us from stopping, taking stock and understanding where we are going and why, until we are interrupted by a catastrophe that brings us stockstill.

If it takes a deadly war for a trauma surgeon to understand what matters most in life, what will it take those of us who dwell in our ivory towers, far away from the brutal realities of daily death and suffering? We, who cling to our earthly possessions as though we will take them with us to the next world, when will we learn to live?

Prioritising material gains over peace and good health when death has the final word is poor logic.

#33
Tact Works!

The employee's face was flushed with emotions as he struggled to come up with a plausible excuse to leave the boss's cabin and answer the "fire brigade" call from his best friend who he knew wouldn't bother him at his work unless it was an emergency.

After a few moments he said, "Sir, it's a call from the new client," then quickly excused himself, "I shall take the call outside."

"Give me your phone. Let me talk to the client," answered the boss.

Thinking quickly, the employee concealed the phone behind his back and responded deferentially, "Sir, why do you want to talk to the client at this stage of the relationship? You are too high up on the ladder to get involved with the deal right now. Let me handle the client at this point and when the deal is almost through, you can speak to them."

Mollified, the boss replied. "Yes, yes, smart thinking. You can take the call outdoors."

All of us have a need for significance and importance, especially those in positions of power. Acknowledge that need appropriately and you will find it much easier to manage superiors.

#34
Growing in Love

On our 20th wedding anniversary, my husband and I decided to go on a date to one of our favourite spots during our courtship – Bandra's famed Bandstand where we used to sit for hours, hand in hand, watching the gorgeous sunset as we threw little stones into the placid water, watching them ripple with a slight splash.

As we settled on the rocks, I was overcome with a sense of serenity. I felt so blessed to have had his strong support throughout the years and thought of how well he had looked after me and the kids.

Our love had only deepened over the years, and it was now as solid as the rock we sat on.

I couldn't help but remember the reckless, wild love of youth we had experienced once upon a time. Then, all that mattered was each other and the rest of the world be damned! There was no simmering stress about whether the kids had eaten their dinner on time, or whether the driver had picked them up from classes on time, or finding the time to make that phone call to the in-law.

Our world has expanded. And fortunately, so has our love.

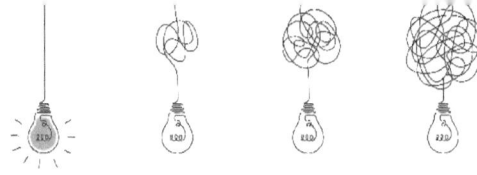

#35
The Greatest Love of All

She applied her make-up like a professional artist and blow-dried her hair with the earnestness of a young girl going on her first date.

As the 50-year-old got ready for an evening out with friends, her adolescent daughter watched and passed a casual remark, removing the earbuds from her ears. "Who are you getting all dolled up for?"

"Why, for myself, of course," the mother remarked, surprised.

The teenager was completely befuddled. She was used to ordering her life around her need to be "accepted" by others. Before attending a party or even a simple outing with friends, she would discuss her outfit with her best friend, taking her advice if it was suitable for the occasion, afraid of standing out like a lotus in a bed of roses.

We must teach our children to be beautiful in their own eyes rather than seek the approval of others.

#36
Kindness: The Supreme Virtue

In the story, Thumbelina keeps the bird warm in the winter to save him from dying. Her kindness will live on in my heart forever.

Among all virtues, kindness reigns supreme in my soul. I instantly connect with kind people – the guest who calls up the day after the party to thank me for all the trouble I put in to be a good host, or an influential elder using his contacts to help me get a job, or a stranger going out of his way to help me locate an address.

Kindness has the power to improve our lives and the lives of others.

When my son told me that kindness was one of my best traits, my heart leaped with joy. I walked up to him and kissed him softly on the cheek. He hugged me and kissed me back.

As Robert Green Ingersoll, a 19th century writer, said, *"Kindness is the sunshine in which virtue grows."*

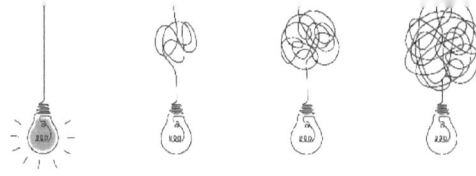

#37
Art Therapy

I was having a bad day after a rather ugly argument with my co-worker, so I decided to cool down by spending some time at an exhibition at the Jehangir Art Gallery in Mumbai. As I walked past the paintings, stopping to take a closer look at some of them, one of the paintings made me stop in my tracks.

It was a sunset painting, and the artist had skilfully depicted the sunset permeating the sky, the clouds, and the surrounding ambience, in warm hues of orange, red, and yellow. The painting evoked feelings of tranquility, awe, and wonder in me.

In that moment, I was transported to one of Goa's beautiful beaches, gazing at the sun going down, and marvelling at the beauty of the natural world. That brief moment served as an escape from the ordinariness of life to something grander and bigger than the wound I had been nursing, which vanished into meaninglessness.

And it dawned on me that any great work of art, whether it be a painting, poetry, movie, a novel, or music, can transport us into another realm. It can renew us and give us a fresh perspective of the wonders of the world, which is still exquisitely cradled in God's love, even when our world may feel like hell on the inside.

What if we took time out each day to appreciate art in all its forms? All our body parts. from head to toe, will find regular rejuvenation and often an escape from the stresses of life

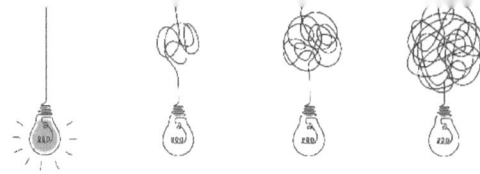

#38
When your Heart Smiles

Have you ever felt your heart truly smile? It is a warm fuzziness like a bird who has escaped from its cage and is basking in the gay warmth of sunshine. It stays with you for a while like a melody that has awoken your senses.

I felt it when a loved one who I thought had abandoned me without explanation, reached out to me through a letter after a few days, and when my teenage son – who I was missing terribly – brought me a special sweetmeat while on his school trip to Rajasthan. It happened again when my husband returned home after a month from an official trip abroad.

I was so happy that I experienced both heaven and earth all at once.

Stay where your heart smiles.

#39
The Walking Dead

With her mother's complete consent, a very brave and daring 17-year-old Afghan girl attempted a precarious solo crossing from Turkey to Spain in a crammed boat, to pursue her passionate dream of becoming an astronaut. Tragically, her overcrowded boat, full of fleeing refugees, capsized, sinking her and her hopes at one go. A few months earlier, this brave heart had suffered a brutal shot in the leg during one of her daredevil attempts to escape to her dreamland, but it only served to ignite her desperation to touch the shores of Spain.

Her story prompted me to reflect on how some people display great courage and live life fearlessly on their own terms, ready to chase what they want while others merely exist in time and space, cocooned in their small, self-contained and caged world, paralysed by fear.

For instance, despite being a father of two lovely children at the age of 45, a friend of mine is racked by fear and anxiety, and bereft of any dream or ambition. He refuses to work for fear that his moderate leg weakness may worsen with travel and exertion, rendering him immobile for the rest of her life. This is despite the fact that the doctor has given her a clean chit to return to work.

He finds no joy in taking his children on vacations to different places in India or overseas, preferring reluctantly to take them to picnic sites that are hourly getaways from Mumbai.

And if you ask him to do anything that threatens to get him out of his comfort zone such as going for an impromptu dinner with a long-lost friend, he will honestly swear that he would rather stay home and do what he enjoys most – rest his legs.

If faced with a domestic problem, he will take his time to solve it. And if you question him, he'll reply, "Take it easy, I am going with the flow," which means he will never resolve the situation but instead put off doing, and eventually put off living.

"Even dead wood floats on water," I reason.

In my mind, the Afghan girl is more alive than he is.

#40
Chocolate Friendship

I reconnected with my old friend, Sapna Mirpuri, after more than 20 years. During that period, we had grown physically apart, and our lives had taken diverse turns. While I married and remained in Mumbai, she emigrated to the United States following her marriage.

So I was delighted to receive an unexpected phone call from her one day informing me that she was in Mumbai. The sad part, though, was that she was nursing a fractured knee she had sustained in a freak accident in Bangalore. She had had knee surgery and was now in the process of healing.

I met her soon. Remarkably, time had little impact on the strength of our friendship as we bonded instantaneously, and the old friendship gradually came back to life through time. Over steaming cups of coffee, we exchanged details of our new lives and the influences moulding them, and we regained the trust and understanding we had had in our late 20s.

We would speak our hearts out, read each other's tone and body language, laugh heartily, and really enjoy each other's company every time we met.

We sought each other's advice, shared secrets, swore confidentiality, and created unforgettable moments. We did not disagree but recognised and accepted our differences. We had no expectations, other than to serve as each other's sounding boards while we tried to make sense of our worlds across space and time.

Many of my current friendships, both old and new, lack this depth and authenticity, being centred on newspaper headlines, office politics, pandemic worries, the art of bringing up children, cuisine, and cooking – information that I can get on the Internet. It is chatting without revealing too many personal facts – a veil of secrecy maintained at all times.

These friendships all appear to be vanilla ice-cream with a chocolate coating on the outside. When all I want is true chocolate ice cream with no boring vanilla.

Seeing her again reminded me that there are friends in life, and then there are friends for life. You can tell the difference when your heart begins to sing each time you meet.

#41
When a soul mate dies

Evon Mascarenhas is 92 years old and lives in London. She lost her loving husband, a renowned journalist who died from a major heart attack at the age of 58, shortly before a planned heart surgery. As the wife of an award-winning journalist she has plenty of stories to tell, which can turn your hours into minutes. She tells vivid anecdotes about sleeping late at night to keep her husband company while he sat on his typewriter.

She describes her social interactions with powerful people as her husband's beautiful wife, and how he could whip up a delicious Chinese feast for his friends in a matter of an hour while she laid out the table, by his side.

When her husband died, her world was shattered. She was like a kitten, lost in the wilderness, crying out for someone to help her. Despite the fact that the marriage was blessed with five lovely children, all of whom were doing well for themselves, she found it exceedingly difficult to cope without him. But – and here's the happy ending – she found her own method of staying sane, and rebuilding her life.

She immersed herself in the love of family and friends while keeping his memory alive by never leaving a conversation without mentioning him. She worked hard to stay in good physical form by exercising and eating the right foods, and kept her spirits up even when smothered in despair.

By refusing to wallow in self-pity, and staying positive, she gradually bloomed like a rose in early summer. Her world was bathed in sunlight; every cloud that passed overhead was nothing but a temporary shadow in her life.

At the age of 92, this wonderful lady is up early every morning, bright like London's beautiful sunshine in summer, to water her pretty little garden. With a watering can in hand, she moves methodically from one flowerbed to the next, devotedly giving each plant a sprinkling. She says she loves seeing leaves and flowers sparkling with fresh water because it gives her a new lease on life every day.

Evon's life is a prime example of how, when life pushes you to the edge of the cliff, you must learn how to let your soul fly.

#42
Happy Relationships Are an Inside Job

I noticed a couple was exploring the glam make-up section of a famous clothing store. They wouldn't have caught my eye if they hadn't had vitiligo, a skin condition that causes white patches on the body.

As the lady picked up two lipsticks off the shelf and the man tested the perfumes on his wrist, they seemed so much happier than the others in the shop. They talked animatedly to one another and smiled a lot, not at all embarrassed or out of place in a huge department store's make-up section.

It was clear that they had become so comfortable in their skin, that it did not matter to them if others thought their appearance odd, or felt sorry for them. They didn't seem to need anyone's approval, quite unlike so many other couples today who keep flaunting their "perfect lives" on Facebook and Instagram, quite often to conceal their less than perfect reality. .

This couple was stunning in their self-assurance.

They were proof that it is irrelevant how the rest of the world perceives you. What counts is how you see yourself.

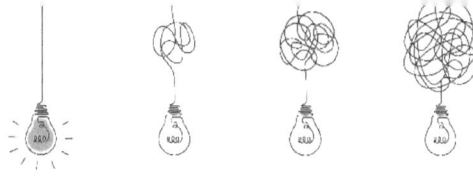

#43
A Make-believe World

The other day I observed my 18-year-old son playing an online game with about 18 other players – some known and others from some part of the world. He had never met them, and would never meet them in his lifetime. His eyes were glued on the screen, his body was moving forward and he swung between elation and rage as his team won or lost to the opposition. At one point I could even hear him scream and grit his teeth in frustration when he was brutally trounced in the game.

I marvelled at the spectacle of a game being played in solitude on a computer box and causing such a stir.

I felt like a ghost from the past as I remembered the good old days when I laughed just like he was doing now but with friends who were actually there as we played kitty kitty, jumped on each other's backs, screamed and collapsed to the ground with our arms spread wide when knackered.

To me, this online game seemed ghostly and so far away from reality. I thought to myself: 'Surely, this cannot be for real. It was a made-up, make-belief, world constructed by technology."

Technology merely serves as a support system for humans. Let's stop making it our reality.

#44
Excuse Me, Please

The authority figure who barged into the room and failed to tell you that the meeting had already started when he knew you were waiting outside, unsure of the venue.

The HR recruiter who said she would get back to you with an offer letter in three days and ignored your follow-ups emails, leaving you in the dark

The invitees at an intimate house party who strolled in two hours late without so much as a prior notice or apology, despite the invitation indicating the time.

As I reflect on these incidents that have left a foul taste in my mouth, the words "If only" flash over my head like a neon sign.

"If only" they had shown some courtesy, the impression they left on me would have been different.

People who fail to show courtesy because they believe it weakens and undermines them, don't realise how much trust, respect and affection they forfeit. In the ultimate analysis, our greatest joy and even success hinges upon our bonds with others. Without a network of loving relationships, our lives are arid and empty, no matter how much money we have.

Courtesy is just polite and pleasant behaviour that shows respect for other people.

Nothing is really gained by not being kind and courteous but a lot is lost.

#45
Pigeons Outside My Window

When we encounter our everyday 'little battles' in life, such as the unfair boss at work, the wicked relative who spreads untruths, or the onset of a sudden illness, we desperately want the universe to lend us a helping hand.

At sad times like these, I usually look outside my window at the pigeons perched on the marble slab outside, eating the grains I've stored in a bowl so lovingly.

The pigeons make no noise, and their silence is a great source of support for me. It reminds me of their unwavering loyalty as a result of the grains provided to them.

The universe often communicates with us in subtle ways, even through the sound of silence.

#46
Lukewarm, not OK, Please

Many parts of the world are experiencing blazing summer heat every year. Wildfires are wreaking havoc in some parts of Canada; Vietnam authorities are forced to put out street lights and ration electricity to stop people from using air conditioners which can start fires.

While efforts are being made to counter climate change, it is just not enough. Lukewarm, at the most.

Come to think of it, lukewarm is the standard temperature of the vast swathe of humanity. We respond tepidly not just to the environment challenge, but to the resolution of our personal problems, or in promoting our favourite cause.

Why are we lukewarm? Why do we have a "chalta hai" mindset, blowing neither hot nor cold?

There are a number of reasons for this half-hearted approach including low self-esteem, laziness, or unresolved emotional or mental traumas.

If we work on our inner healing, we will, in time, grow in confidence, strength and self-belief. As we do so, our inner temperature of commitment and conviction grows and enables us to infuse all our activities with passion and care. In time, we will start to believe we have the capacity within us to alter our environment and make it a better place for our children.

We should fight for the change we want to see.

#47
Let it Be

I visited my 80-year-old, widowed aunt at an old age home in Mumbai, run by Catholic nuns. She had decided to move into the home despite being in good health and leading a comfortable life flanked by loving neighbours and friends who dropped by periodically.

All of us were unhappy with her decision to trade her independence and a lovely home in exchange for living with more than 70 inmates, some of whom were very old and feeble. I had advised her to remain in her own home and hire a full-time maid to cook her meals and tend to all her needs. But she adhered to her decision. She didn't want to be a burden to anyone or be dictated to by maids. Nor did she want neighbours, friends, or family to worry about her constantly since she was starting to forget things.

When I visited her after a few months, she looked fragile. Age had caught up with her and she appeared to have resigned to the 'fate', which she herself had chosen for herself. She wasn't the same person I knew who used to crack jokes, make and pour us a cup of tea despite being slow on her feet, and tell us endless tales about her life.

She admitted she was becoming even more forgetful, didn't have any real friends, and that the food was just basic. On the bright side, she was glad that she didn't have to cook any meals, was looked after, and spent the majority of the day sleeping, reading or going on walks. Although she missed her home, she still did not regret her decision.

But from my perspective, it seemed that from being in control of her own life, she had to abide by others' rules and regulations. From having well-wishers who lovingly cared for her, she had sterile hands who took care of her. From being in a happy environment, she was now in a hapless one. She had wilfully accelerated her aging process.

I felt miserable after seeing her.

Sometimes we take decisions without fully comprehending their repercussions, and often lack the flexibility, especially as we age, to retrace our steps. Thus, we let slip our hold on happiness. And at such times, there is nothing anyone else can do.

Unfortunately, there are times when you simply have to let things be.

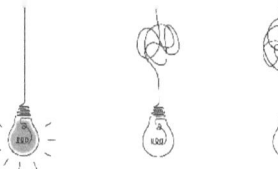

#48
Learning to Let Go

Her son will soon join medical school and she knows his life will now take on a new shape and substance. No longer will he be the little sun her life revolved around. She enjoyed being a mother to him. She loved serving him his meals on time and watching him relish them. She felt victorious that the home environment was just perfect for him to study for his entrance exams. She enjoyed their impromptu discussions about nothing at all. Suddenly, she felt bereaved; that something valuable was being stolen from her. Her heart ached with the thought of how lonely she would be without him. She even said, "Hey, I am coming with you!", forgetting for a moment she had her husband and daughter to look after.

Tears welled in her eyes with pain and fear of separation.

What she didn't realise was that in going two steps ahead, she had failed to experience the pride and joy of his achievement completely. She had relegated that to a second position, which was so unfair to him.

She needed to let him go and let go of him. He had his dreams to live.

But while his wings took flight, she would miss that part of him that had awakened the mother in her.

#49
Double Standards

His eyes were blazing with smouldering rage as he told me how terrible he felt. Not only had he been asked to put in his papers for no fault of his own but they wouldn't even offer him a notice period. This cut like a knife "We're so sorry to let you go immediately, but we simply cannot afford you. We have no complaints against you, and if we could we'd retain you," they said awkwardly.

"But I expected you to give me at least a month's notice," the unfortunate employee said.

"So sorry, but we can no longer afford to tap into our savings," they said, and cut short the conversation.

He felt shocked and betrayed all at once, their justifications for letting him go so easily hanging limply in the air. He recalled how only a few weeks ago, the same leaders were seething with rage when the client servicing manager resigned after the company had achieved a major milestone. "At least he should have given us some notice, how could he just drop out like this?" they had asked, dramatically.

He was astonished by their double standard.

He felt they had treated him with the same lack of integrity that their former client servicing employee had treated them, but they felt justified in doing so since they had good intentions but were in a trap.

Often, we tend to judge others by their behaviour, and ourselves by our intentions.

We focus on the speck in our brother's eye, while oblivious of the log on our own.

#50
Who am I?

I am a wife, mother, sister, and daughter of my deceased parents.

I give equal importance to work and life.

I take care of my body and health.

I am not impractical but strive to find realistically workable solutions to complex problems.

I accept people as they are, but have a soft corner for those who work hard for a living.

I appreciate efforts more than the results.

I hate mistakes because I know a mistake can cost a life. Yet, I eventually forgive myself and others when one is made.

I am still working on being consistently disciplined because I know it's the key to achieving success.

I have so many goals but realise that I only have one body that I need to take care of, so I am patient with myself. I know I will achieve them eventually.

I am still learning to love myself better; love myself perhaps even more than I do my husband and children.

I admire those who dare to be different because they are confident in who they are.

I am not brave like the soldiers on the front line or the doctors battling to save the lives of the almost-dead, but I am brave in the way I handle the challenges and complications of my own little life.

I wish I could do more for the old, sick, and dying.

Sometimes I feel like a lost child among a sea of people.

I am myself, unique, special.

Yet, in all this crowd of identities that comprise me, have I lost the real me?

Reviews

Fr. Antony Charanghat
Editor - The Examiner

The author's enlightening booklet is a heartfelt invitation to explore the deeper facets of life. The author's intent and aspiration is to inspire others to live more meaningful lives that are commendable. Griselda's emphasis on learning from daily happenings and self-reflection resonates as valuable guidance in today's complex world. The offer to include blank pages for readers to contribute their observations adds an interactive dimension to the diary, fostering a sense of community and shared learning.

Mario Poppen
Former Corporate Director - Marketing Alliances and Partnerships for a leading hotel company

This labor of love of Griselda's for her dear parents who were friends and the most genuine well-wishers of my family and me, will resonate with some of you.

Your perusing these reflections and reminiscences, dedicated to paragons, may I hope add to and enrich your experience of all the bounty that we take for granted.

Delight in Griselda's life lessons and suffuse yourself with their joy, quiet lyricism, and sense of fulfillment.

Parneet Kaur

Associate Vice President, Marketing, Sony Pictures Network India and recent BW Marketing World's 'Marketers 40 under 40' awardee

Griselda's writing is brimming with soul and authenticity, a true reflection of her character. As you read her book, her presence permeates every page. Her writing is pure, spirited and pragmatic, stemming from a distinct perspective, which she carries with her like a candle in the dark, illuminating her beautiful mind and thoughts.

Varsha Khanna
Writer & Editor
Ex-Journalist, Features – Business Standard

Within the pages of this self-help book, fashioned in an anecdotal style, Griselda unveils an often counter intuitive perspective on various life events and individuals. Her writing emanates a harmonious blend of humility and ease, equilibrium and grace, empathy, and profound sensitivity.

Annabelle Ferro
Writer & Owner - Deogadh The Homestay

Finding the extra in the ordinary is what Griselda Pinto does in her diary musings called 'Wisdom Shots'. Each of us experience our own 'wisdom shots' everyday. And reading through her insights makes me wonder why we do not take out time to press that pause button and put our thoughts out there. Wisdom abounds everywhere. Life lessons taught - if only we learn them - and share them with the world like Griselda did. And she has thoughtfully left a few blank pages in her book for you to do so!

Notes

Notes

Notes

Notes

Notes

www.ingramcontent.com/pod-product-compliance
Lightning Source LLC
LaVergne TN
LVHW041538070526
838199LV00046B/1718